How Do I Know It's Yucky?

and other questions about the senses

by

Sharon Cromwell

Photographs by

Richard Smolinski, Jr.

Series Consultant

Dan Hogan

RIGBY INTERACTIVE LIBRARY
DES PLAINES, ILLINOIS

02 01 00 99 98
10 9 8 7 6 5 4 3 2 1

Produced by Times Offset (M) Sdn. Bhd.

Library of Congress Cataloging-in-Publication Data

Cromwell , Sharon , 1947-
  How do I know it's yucky? : and other questions about the senses / by Sharon Cromwell ; photographs by Richard Smolinski, Jr .
    p.   cm. -- (Body wise)
  Includes bibliographical references and index.
  Summary: Describes how the five human senses work separately and together and discusses such related topics as brain messages , receptor cells , and sound waves.
    ISBN 1-57572-160-0 (lib. bdg.)
    1. Senses and sensation--Juvenile literature .   [1. Senses and sensation.]
I . Smolinski , Dick , ill .   II. Title .   III. Series .
QP434.C76   1998
612.8--dc21   97-25180
                                                                    CIP
                                                                    AC

Some words are shown in bold, **like this.** You can find out what they mean by looking in the glossary.

Contents

What are my senses?

You have five senses. They are are touch, taste, hearing, sight, and smell.

You have touch receptors, or feelers, all over your body. You taste mostly with your tongue. You hear with your ears. You see with your eyes, and you smell with your nose. Your brain plays a big part in all these things.

HEALTH FACT
You have the most touch receptors in your fingertips. That's why you often touch things with your fingertips.

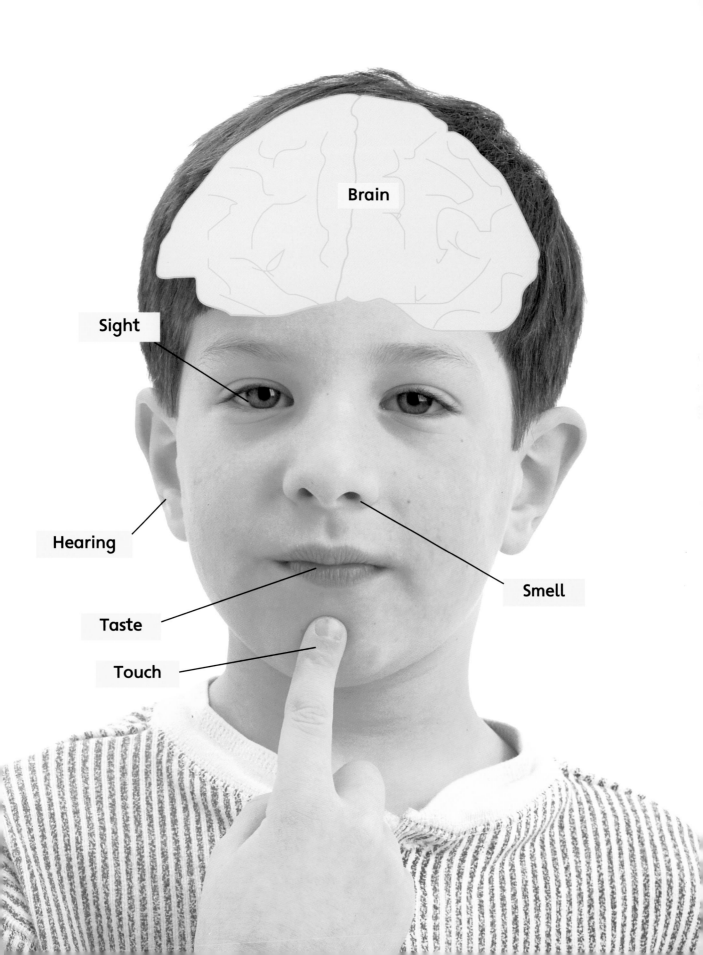

Brain

Sight

Hearing

Smell

Taste

Touch

What do my senses tell me?

Your senses tell you everything about the world around you. Your sense of touch lets you feel things. It also helps keep you safe. If you touch something very hot, you pull away from it. That keeps you from getting burned.

Your sense of hearing also helps to keep you safe. When you hear a car horn, it is often a warning of danger. Hearing also helps you to communicate with others. Your sense of sight lets you see things all around you. This helps you move through your world safely.

HEALTH FACT
Your sense of taste and your sense of smell often work together. They help you decide what you want to eat and whether a food is too sour!

How do I feel something is itchy?

Your whole body is made up of tiny **cells.** Special cells, called receptors, are in your skin. Certain receptor cells feel itching and tickling. Let's call them "feeler" cells.

HEALTH FACT

If your body swells up where you were bitten by an insect, tell a grown-up. You may be **allergic** to the insect bite.

1. You have feeler cells that feel itching all over your body.

2. When your feeler cells feel an itch on your arm or some other part of your body, they send a message through your nerves to your brain.

3. Your brain sends a message to the muscles in your arm and hand.

4. Then you scratch the place that itches.

Feeler cells in the skin

Nerves

Message goes to brain

How do I know my dirty socks smell yucky?

Your nose and your brain work together so you can smell different smells and tell them apart.

HEALTH FACT

You can't always tell if food is **fresh** by its smell. If you are unsure, ask a grown-up.

1. Smells are made up of tiny parts that are called molecules. They enter your nostrils.

2. Inside your nose are millions of feeler **cells** that are sensitive to smells. These cells send a message to the smell center of the brain.

3. The smell center of the brain identifies the smell.

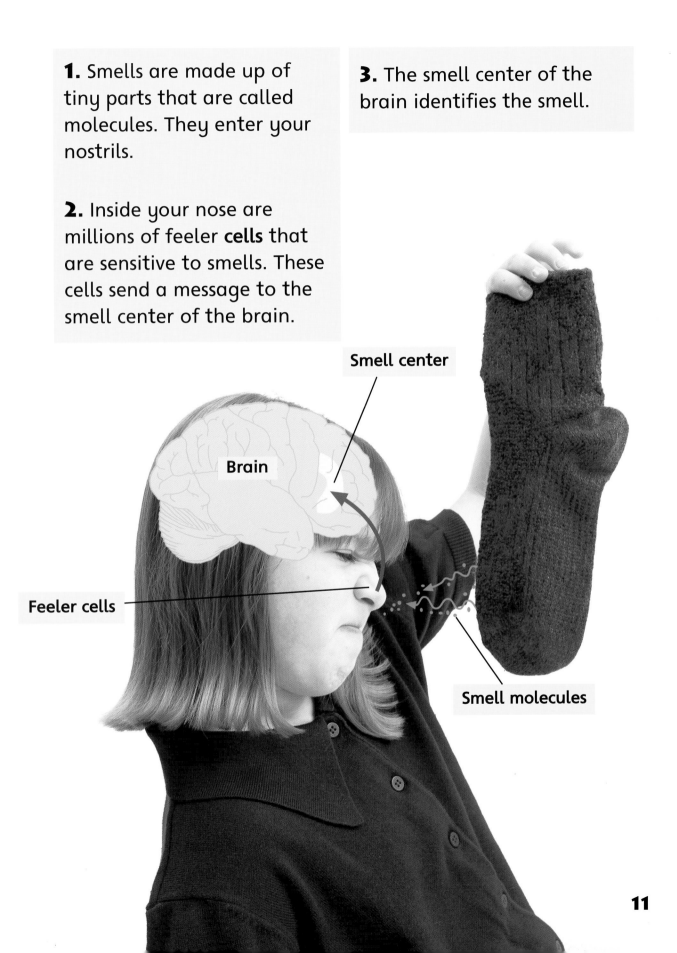

Smell center

Brain

Feeler cells

Smell molecules

How do I know something is too loud?

Sounds make invisible waves in the air. The waves vibrate—or shake—tiny bones in your ears. If a sound causes too much vibration, you know it is too loud.

HEALTH FACT

Levels of sound are measured in units called decibels. A normal tone of voice is about 60 decibels. Sounds over 85 decibels can be harmful to your ears.

1. Sound waves move into your ears and vibrate your eardrums. The eardrum is a thin layer of skin that is stretched like the top of a drum.

2. When your eardrum vibrates, it makes bones in your ear vibrate.

3. The vibrating bones shake up tiny hairs in liquid in your inner ear.

4. Each tiny hair is connected to a nerve ending that sends signals to your brain.

5. When your brain receives these signals, it knows what you are hearing.

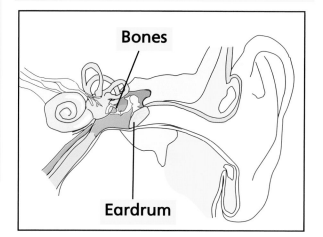

Bones

Eardrum

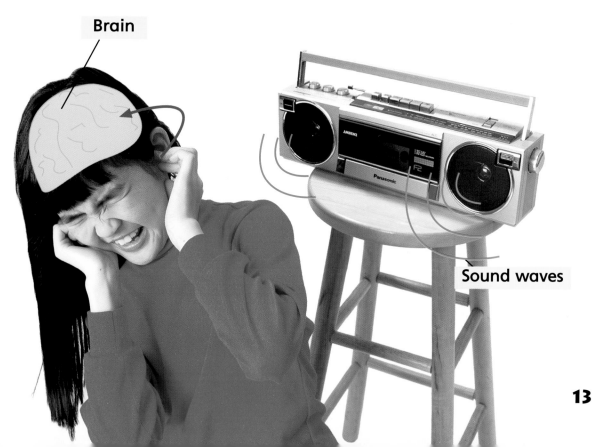

Brain

Sound waves

How do I taste bitter, sweet, salty, and sour foods?

Tiny bumps on your tongue called taste buds let you taste.

HEALTH FACT

Eating cold foods makes your taste buds less sensitive. If you suck on an ice cube before taking some medicine, you won't notice the taste.

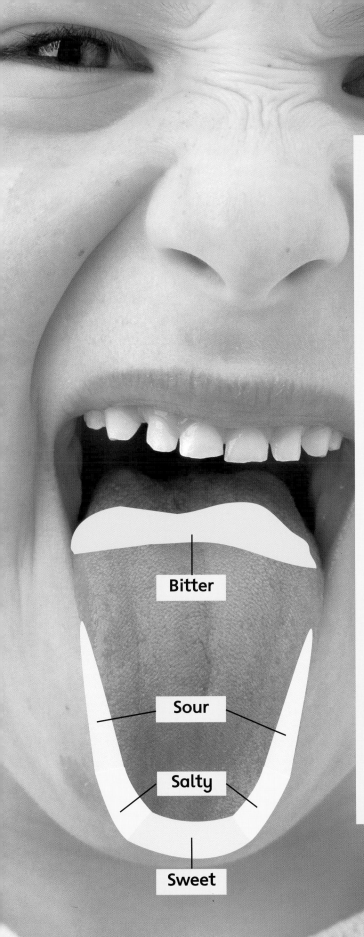

Bitter

Sour

Salty

Sweet

1. Taste buds are made up of feeler **cells** that take in the taste of foods.

2. You have four kinds of taste buds. These taste buds know whether something is sweet, sour, salty, or bitter.

3. When you chew food your taste buds are **activated** by different foods that taste sweet, sour, salty, or bitter. So if you eat something salty, like a potato chip, the "salt taste buds" work.

4. The taste buds send messages to your brain that you are eating something salty.

5. Your brain then knows what you are eating.

Why can't I taste food when I have a cold?

It is hard to taste food when you have a cold because the senses of taste and smell work together.

HEALTH FACT

When you have a cold, try taking a hot shower to clear your nose. You will be better able to taste your food.

1. The stuffy nose that you often have with a cold makes it difficult to smell.

2. Your taste buds detect only four simple tastes of salty, sweet, bitter, and sour. Your nose and sense of smell do much of the rest of the work of tasting!

3. The smell molecules from food give your brain much of the information it needs to identify the food.

4. When you can't smell the many **aromas** of food, you lose much of your ability to taste it.

Brain

Smell molecules

How do I know whether something is rough or smooth?

Feeler cells in your fingertips help you feel whether an object is rough or smooth.

1. Feeler **cells** in your fingertips feel texture— whether something is rough or smooth. Your hand has more feeler cells than most parts of your body.

2. When you touch an object, a message about its texture goes from your feeler cells through your nerves to your brain.

3. Your brain tells you whether the object is rough or smooth.

4. If it is rough, like sandpaper, you will probably pull your hand away. If the object is soft and silky, like the fur on a pet animal, you may decide to stroke it.

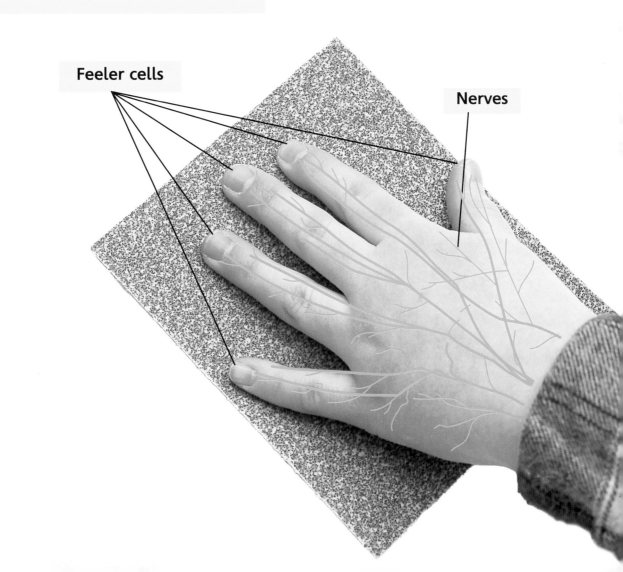

Feeler cells

Nerves

How do my eyes see color?

Two kinds of light receptors are at the back of your eyes. One kind of light receptor takes in color.

HEALTH FACT

Cantaloupe, carrots, and other orange-colored fruits and vegetables have an important vitamin called vitamin A. It helps your eyes to see when the light is poor.

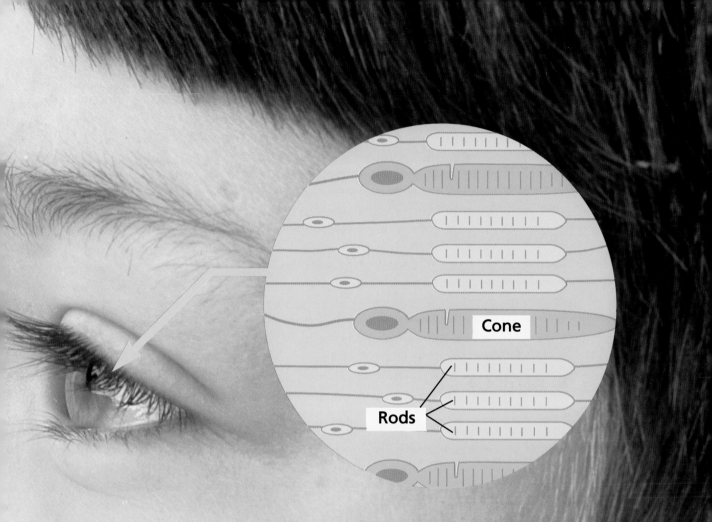

Cone

Rods

1. The two kinds of light receptors at the back of your eyes are called rods and cones. All together, the human eye has about 135 million rods and cones.

2. Rods are **cells** that are sensitive to light and dark. Three kinds of cones are receptor cells for three different colors.

3. One kind of cone receives red. Another kind receives blue. The third kind receives green.

4. Messages to the brain from the three kinds of cones combine to make all the colors you see. You can see millions of colors, all made up from those red, blue, and green receiving cones.

EXPLORE MORE!
Your Senses

1. GET TOUCHY!
WHAT YOU'LL NEED:
- water
- ice cubes
- 2 containers

THEN TRY THIS!
Pour water and some ice cubes into one container. Stir them until the water is very cold. Put some cool water in a second container. Put your hand in the ice water and leave it there as you count to 20. Take your hand out and put it into the cool water. What does the cool water feel like? Compared to ice-cold water, cool water feels warm.

2. IN GOOD TASTE!
WHAT YOU'LL NEED:
- salt
- 8-ounce glass of water

THEN TRY THIS!
Put 2 teaspoons of salt in an 8-ounce glass of water. Then put some salty water on the back of your tongue. Next put some salty water on the front. How did the salty water taste on the back of your tongue? How did it taste on the front? Can you tell which part of your tongue has your salt taste buds?

3. FAIR HEARING

WHAT YOU'LL NEED:

- a rubber band
- an empty tissue box

THEN TRY THIS!
This activity will show you a little bit about sound.

Stretch the rubber band around the tissue box. (This rubber band is like your eardrum.) Then pluck the band once with your forefinger. The air around the rubber band will vibrate. At some point, the band will stop moving. Was the sound from the band louder when it first started to vibrate or louder when it had almost stopped?

4. GET NOSY

WHAT YOU'LL NEED:

- a few bites of a food you like

THEN TRY THIS!
Take a bite of the food. Think about how it tastes. Then pinch your nose between your finger and your thumb, and eat another bite of food. How does it taste now? How does smelling affect the way your food tastes?

Glossary

activate To cause to work.

allergic Likely to become swollen, develop a rash, or sneeze a lot because of an insect bite, food, or substance in the air.

aromas Smells.

cells Very small parts of a person, animal, or plant.

elements Simple or basic parts.

fresh Unspoiled; not old.

More Books to Read

Berry, Joy W. *Teach Me about Tasting.* Danbury, CT: Grolier Inc., 1993.

Carratello, Patricia and John Carratello. *Let's Investigate the Senses.* Westminster, CA: Teacher Created Materials, 1984.

Cole, Joanna. *You Can't Smell a Flower with Your Ear! All about Your 5 Senses.* New York: Putnam Publishing Group, 1994.

McMillan, Bruce. *Sense Suspense.* New York: Scholastic, Inc., 1994.

Otto, Carolyn. *I Can Tell By Touching.* New York: HarperCollins Children's Books, 1994.

Index